First Facts®

The Solar System

Mercury

by Adele Richardson

Consultant:
Stephen J. Kortenkamp, PhD
Research Scientist
Planetary Science Institute, Tucson, Arizona

Capstone
press®

Mankato, Minnesota

First Facts is published by Capstone Press,
151 Good Counsel Drive, P.O. Box 669, Mankato, Minnesota 56002.
www.capstonepress.com

Library of Congress Cataloging-in-Publication Data
Richardson, Adele, 1966–
    Mercury / by Adele Richardson.—Rev. and updated.
    p. cm.—(First facts. The Solar system)
    Includes bibliographical references and index.
    ISBN-13: 978-1-4296-0724-7 (hardcover)
    ISBN-10: 1-4296-0724-6 (hardcover)
    1. Mercury (Planet)—Juvenile literature. I. Title. II. Series.
QB611.R53 2008
523.41—dc22   2007003525

Summary: Discusses the orbit, surface features, and exploration of the planet Mercury.

Editorial Credits

Christopher Harbo, editor; Juliette Peters, designer and illustrator; Jo Miller, photo researcher;
    Scott Thoms, photo editor

Photo Credits

Astronomical Society of the Pacific/NASA, 14–15
NASA/The Johns Hopkins University Applied Physics Laboratory, 17
NASA/JPL/Northwestern University, 5, 9, 20
Photodisc, cover, 1, 4, planet images within illustrations and chart, 7, 11, 13, 19, 21
Space Images/NASA/JPL, 10
Steven L. Kipp, 16

1 2 3 4 5 6 12 11 10 09 08 07

Table of Contents

Mariner 10 and Mercury

Mercury has been visited by only one spacecraft. *Mariner 10* took pictures of the planet in 1974. The pictures showed a rocky ball covered with **craters**. Scientists thought Mercury looked like Earth's moon.

Fast Facts about Mercury

Diameter: 3,031 miles (4,878 kilometers)

Average Distance from Sun: 36 million miles (58 million kilometers)

Average Temperature (at surface): 801 degrees Fahrenheit (427 degrees Celsius) during the day; minus 279 degrees Fahrenheit (minus 173 degrees Celsius) at night.

Length of Rotation: 59 Earth days

Length of Day: 176 Earth days

Length of Year: 88 Earth days

Moons: None

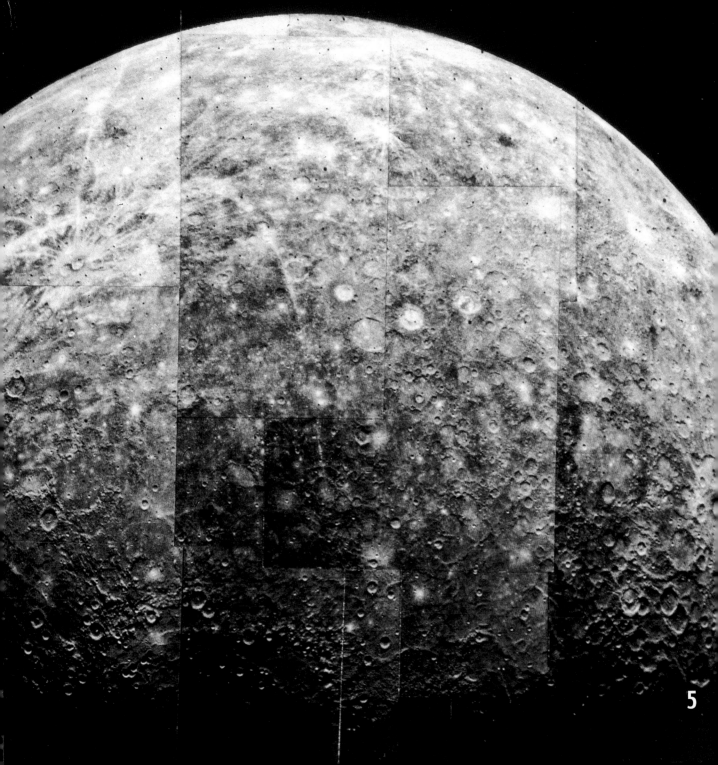

5

The Solar System

Mercury is the closest planet to the Sun. Venus, Earth, and Mars are the next closest. These planets are mostly made of rock. Jupiter, Saturn, Uranus, and Neptune are the next farthest planets. They are made of gas and ice.

Sun

Mercury

Venus

Earth

Moon

Mars

Jupiter

Saturn

Uranus

Neptune

7

Mercury's Lack of Atmosphere

An **atmosphere** is a layer of gases that surrounds a planet. Mercury has no atmosphere. Any gases around Mercury escape into space. Without an atmosphere, the planet's surface is very hot during the day. Mercury's surface is very cold at night.

⏱ Fun Fact!
With no atmosphere, Mercury's sky always looks black, even during the day.

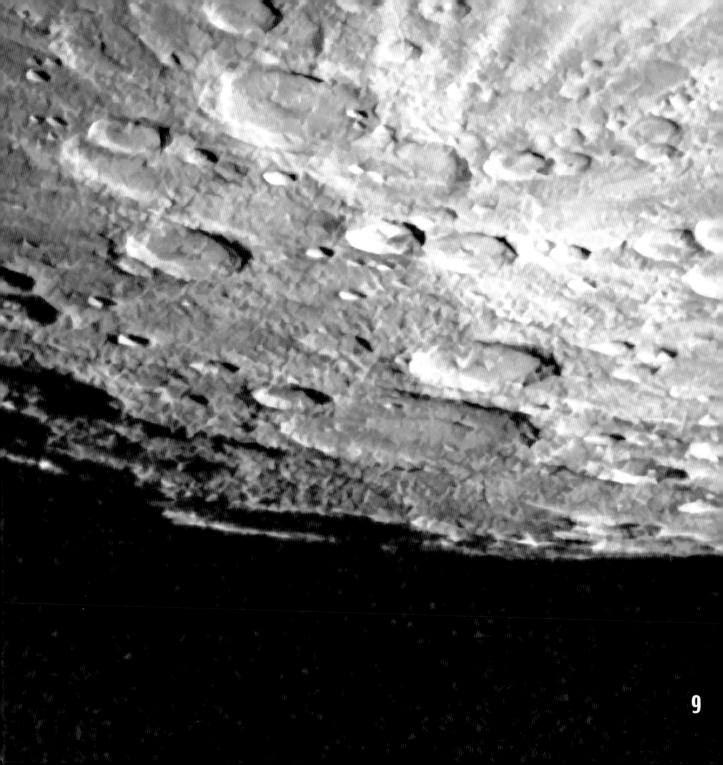

9

Mercury's Makeup

Mercury is made mostly of rock. Its **crust**, or surface, is covered with craters, cliffs, and hills. A rocky **mantle** lies below the crust.

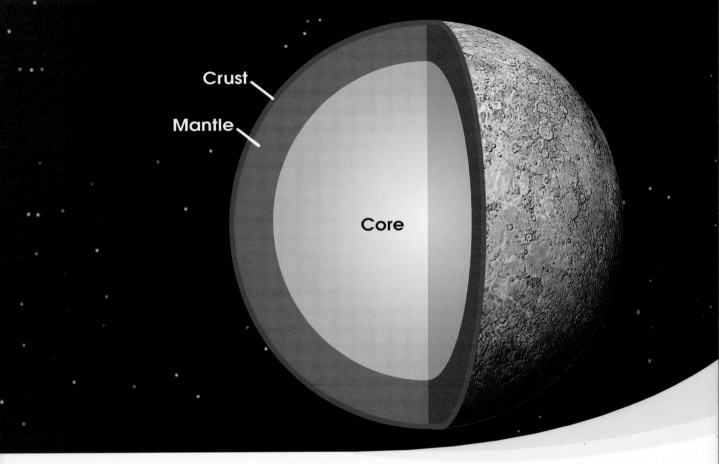

Crust

Mantle

Core

Mercury has a solid iron **core**.
The core makes up most of the planet.
Scientists believe a very thin layer of
melted iron may surround the core.

How Mercury Moves

Mercury moves in two ways. It quickly circles around the Sun. It also slowly spins on its **axis**. Mercury takes 88 Earth days to circle the Sun once. This period of time is Mercury's year. It takes 59 Earth days to spin around on its axis once.

Fun Fact!
Because Mercury spins so slowly, one day on Mercury (sunrise to sunrise) lasts 176 Earth days. On Mercury, a day is twice as long as a year.

Sun

Mercury

Path around the Sun

Axis

Caloris Basin

The Caloris Basin is a giant crater on Mercury. It is about 810 miles (1,300 kilometers) wide. Scientists believe the crater was made when an **asteroid** smashed into Mercury. The crash also formed hills and mountains.

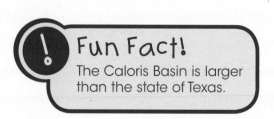

Fun Fact!
The Caloris Basin is larger than the state of Texas.

Edge of Caloris Basin

15

Studying Mercury

Mercury is hard to see from Earth. The planet appears low in the sky just before sunrise or just after sunset. People use telescopes to see Mercury at these times.

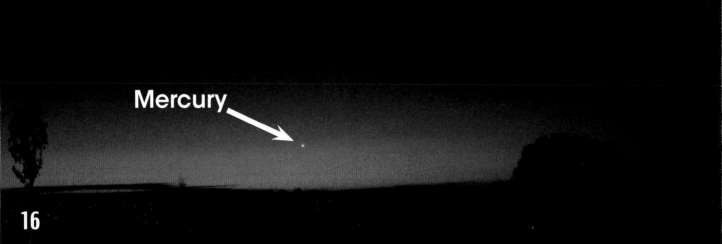

Mercury

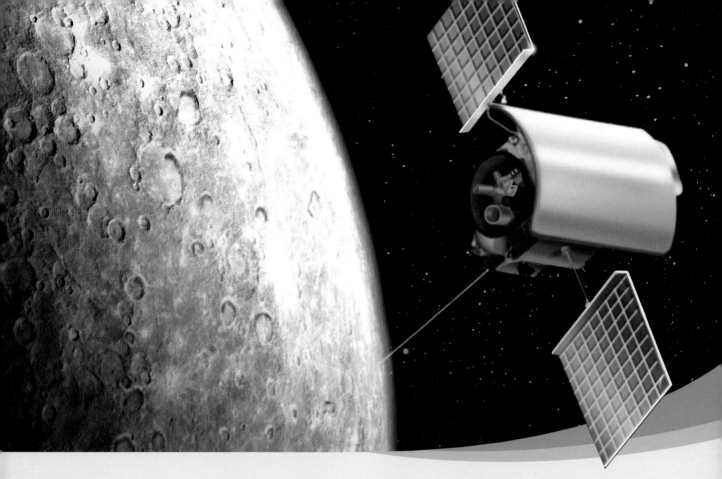

Scientists use spacecraft to study Mercury. The *Messenger* spacecraft will arrive at Mercury in 2011. *Messenger* will circle the planet for one Earth year.

Comparing Mercury to Earth

Mercury and Earth are very different. People could not breathe on Mercury. The planet does not have an atmosphere. People could not live on Mercury either. Its temperatures are too hot during the day and too cold at night.

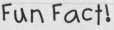 **Fun Fact!**
Jupiter and Saturn each have a moon that is bigger than Mercury.

Size Comparison

Earth

Mercury

Amazing but True!

Mercury is a wrinkled planet. Its core was once hotter than it is today. As the core cooled, the planet shrank. Mercury's surface cracked and wrinkled like a raisin. Cliffs and ridges formed on the surface.

Planet Comparison

Planet	Size Rank (1=largest)	Makeup	1 Trip around the Sun (Earth Time)
Mercury	8	rock	88 days
Venus	6	rock	225 days
Earth	5	rock	365 days, 6 hours
Mars	7	rock	687 days
Jupiter	1	gases and ice	11 years, 11 months
Saturn	2	gases and ice	29 years, 6 months
Uranus	3	gases and ice	84 years
Neptune	4	gases and ice	164 years, 10 months

Glossary

asteroid (ASS-tuh-roid)—a large rocky body that moves around the Sun; asteroids are too small to be called planets.

atmosphere (AT-muhss-feehr)—the layer of gases that surrounds some planets and moons

axis (AK-siss)—an imaginary line that runs through the middle of a planet; a planet spins on its axis.

core (KOR)—the inner part of a planet that is made of metal or rock

crater (KRAY-tur)—a hole made when an asteroid or a large piece of rock crashes into a planet or moon

crust (KRUHST)—the thin outer layer of a planet's surface

mantle (MAN-tuhl)—the part of a planet between the crust and the core

Read More

Dunn, Mary R. *A Look at Mercury.* Astronomy Now. New York: Rosen, 2008.

Orme, Helen, and David Orme. *Let's Explore Mercury.* Space Launch! Milwaukee: Gareth Stevens, 2007.

Taylor-Butler, Christine. *Mercury.* Scholastic News Nonfiction Readers. New York: Children's Press, 2007.

Internet Sites

FactHound offers a safe, fun way to find Internet sites related to this book. All of the sites on FactHound have been researched by our staff.

Here's how:
1. Visit *www.facthound.com*
2. Choose your grade level.
3. Type in this book ID **1429607246** for age-appropriate sites. You may also browse subjects by clicking on letters, or by clicking on pictures and words.
4. Click on the **Fetch It** button.

FactHound will fetch the best sites for you!

Index